Copyright © 2025 Optimum Vizhan

All rights reserved. No part of this publication may be reproduced, stored in retrieval system, or transmitted, in any form or by any means, electronic, mechanical, photocopying, recording, or otherwise, without the written prior permission of the author.

ISBN: 979-8-9921415-7-3 Kindle.
ISBN: 979-8-9921415-8-0 Paper.

Library of Congress Control Number: 1-14626829121

Because of the dynamic nature of the internet, any web addresses or links contained in this book may have changed since the publication and may no longer be valid. The views expressed in this work are solely those of the author and do not necessarily reflect the views of the publisher, and the publisher hereby disclaims any responsibility for them.

OV-MAX PUBLISHING (DATE: 12-04-2024)
Cover Design By: Optimum Vizhan
LOGO OV-MAX PUBLISHING www.optimumvizhan.com/ovmaxpublishing

North America & International: support@ov-max.com

CONTENTS

Copyright	
DISCLAIMER	1
TRIBUTE TO MAX	2
PREFACE	5
The Rosetta Stone of Unconditional Love:	7
The Rosetta Stone of Unconditional Love Fundamental Components for one Person.	18
The Rosetta Stone of Unconditional Love Fundamental Components for Up to Five People	34
HOW TO DISCOVER MY TWO DOMINATE CHARACTERISTICS	36
HOW TO DISCOVER MY MAJOR AND MINOR CHARACTERISTICS	38
MAJOR AND MINOR CHARACTERISTICS COMBOS	40
HOW TO DISCOVER MY MACRO AND MICRO CHARACTERISTICS	46
MAXIMIZING ORGANIZATION'S POTENTIAL	48
FRONT COVER	50
BACK COVER	51
In Closing	52
About The Author	53

the ROSETTA STONE *Of* Unconditional Love

DISCLAIMER

The Rosetta Stone of Unconditional Love *is not* an artifact; and or actual stone with inscriptions on it, referring to Unconditional Love. The Rosetta Stone of Unconditional Love; is the components of Unconditional Love, arranged in a pattern. This pattern allows the individual to self-diagnosis themselves; in finding out where they are at being at peace, with themselves in and with the Unconditional Love part of the Spirit.

The Rosetta Stone of Unconditional Love does not help self-centered love people; who enjoy being self-centered, regardless. Read more in the book ETENALIZING CREATION Final Phase.

It might only reveal proof of self-centered love, by how the person reacts to specific questions. If so; then might be best to stop the session, and or skip over to avoid conflicts.

TRIBUTE TO MAX

Maximus is looking out in the distance. This photo was taken about two months before his transitioning on. This photo was taken from the video version. I was drawn to take this video; not knowing that Max was preparing us, for this next phase of our friendship...

The video starts out with Max laying on the ground. He normally lays on the ground to scratch his back; to do the back stroke, as though he was swimming in water. This time nothing. Then he pops up and takes his front right paw; and digs in the loose dirt, with one stroke. He usually starts digging a hole. Sniffs the dirt or something else, but never has he just did a one stroke dig. Then looks up and walks along the fence line; and looks out into the distance, like he Is seeing something grand and spiritual...

A day or two after Max had transitioned on; missing him like no other, I looked at all the videos and photos of Max. I took over the years. As I was watching this video; as I just described above. It became crystal clear; Max was letting me know. He was going to lie down; I would have to dig a hole, for his physical body. Then we would move forward; together in our friendship, in starting this Final Phase of Eternalizing Creation...

I got goose bumps on my tingling sensations; all over my body when I was experiencing this revelation, for the first time. It was fitting. Max from day one of our friendship; was always positioning us, for the events that were about to transpire...

He was gently conditioning me all that time. To prepare me for this **BIG** one; in him transitioning on, so that we can work together on both sides spiritually and physically. Together, guiding and assisting all creation in this Final Phase of Eternalizing Creation...

Again Max, *Thank You sooooo Much for Your Beyond Epic Friendship! Seriously Bro!!*

It's been an Honor and Privilege to have this vision, experiences
with my Bestest Friend in All of Creation,

"Maximus Houdini Koan."

THANK YOU, MAX!

MILLIONS. SERIOUSLY.

This Journey with You has been priceless,

is priceless and no doubt will continue to be priceless.

I Love You Maximus Houdini Koan

with all My Spirit, Mind and Body!

I AM SO … SO VERY PROUD OF YOU!

It's an Honor and Privilege to be
On this Journey with You.
FROM THE BEGINNING WHEN
The Unconditional Love part of Spirit Created Us,
To Now and Beyond!!!

You and Me
Forever BEST Friends!
In Pure Unconditional Love!!

Those prior words that are in bold; were the same words I would say to Max, while gently holding his face with both of my hands.

PREFACE

Welcome to the Rosetta Stone of Unconditional Love. Finally. Lol. No long intros like in the book Eternalizing Creation Final Phase. But a tribute to the book Eternalizing Creation Final Phase; for introducing to the World, the Rosetta Stone of Unconditional Love. **THANK YOU, TONS!**

This book serves as a Self-Help Manual, in understanding the five characteristics of Unconditional Love. Plus, there macros and micros.

This Self-Help Manual explains how we can discover; which two of the five characteristics are dominate in my personal spirit, mind and body. And how I can see and understand, what other peoples dominate two characteristics are.

Then wrap it all up with the understanding; *where I am at peace* with Unconditional Love in my life, on the Rosetta Stone of Unconditional Love. Those areas I'm at peace with, I can celebrate knowing without a shadow of doubt. Those areas I'm not; I can go right to work on them, in becoming at peace them as well.

***We've included the one and only*...** the Rosetta Stone of Unconditional Love diagram; to use as a worksheet, to get us use to it and how it works. This Rosetta Stone of Unconditional Love can be used by One Person; and or up to Five People, for Individual Study, Small Family or Groups.

Plus, Two Characteristic Tables of the Unconditional Love part of the Spirit.

This is truly a Key to Unlocking Restoration in my life, my relationships and with the Unconditional Love part of the Spirit.

Welcome to the Final Phase...

Enjoy!

Without further due, let's get started.

THE ROSETTA STONE OF UNCONDITIONAL LOVE:

Yup. This Spiritual Artifact was hidden all this time. And it was only to be discovered during the Final Phase.

If you want all the details of the whys; then it would be best understood in the book, Eternalizing Creation Final Phase.

The short version is... this was a learning curve for humans; in wanting to understand the five words the Unconditional Love part of the Spirit was referencing to, but they did not understand. The only way we could learn the meaning of these words; was experiencing them the hard way, in our physical bodies.

These five words are: faith, perseverance, compassion, forgiveness and peace. The Unconditional Love part of the Spirit was feeling all these, when it was creating its eternal friends (all of creation) from thoughts, to created thoughts (spirits), to their physical bodies and their eternal physical bodies.

Oops, I said short version. Ok a tad more...

All of creation wanted to know so bad, they **All** agreed to be physically created. **Yup. Spoiler.**

Having the five physical senses; would help them understand these words, to their/our cores. These five words are the five characteristics of Unconditional Love. These five characteristics *is what drove* the Unconditional Love part of the Spirit to create Eternal Friends...

There are Five Phases in Creating Eternal Friends; that will 100% make all of its creation, uniquely like the Unconditional Love part of the Spirit. They/we will all be in one spirit, mind and body. Both/All will understand each other clearly; and *completely* enjoy their friendship/s, throughout all eternity...

Ok. I could keep going on; but this short summary will end up be a whole big chapter, because I like to talk and write. Lol.

Again; to better appreciate the Rosetta Stone of Unconditional Love, one needs to read and become apart of the Journey in Eternalizing Creation Final Phase. *With heavy emphasis on **appreciate**.*

Unconditional Love Spirit part of the Spirit is composed, of five major characteristics. Each characteristic has five components. ***When We become at peace*** with all five components; with each of the five characteristics Unconditional Love part of the Spirit. Then we can go to the nth level in our friendship, with the "Creator" the Unconditional Love part of the Spirit. SERIOUSLY.

THE FIVE CHARACTERISTICS OF UNCONDITIONAL LOVE:

Note: Read and Absorb These in Baby Steps. *Hmm.* Maybe that's why started out as babies. So that we would pace ourselves; the same way, throughout our whole life journey. *Spoiler 2.0*

1st FAITH: Requires INSIGHT. Seeing. Insights of Doing Something without any prior knowledge and training.

Tad Deeper. Insight is the Core of Faith. Deeper. Faith is the Core of Insight.

Thus, physical sight. One must see the desired physical results, to encourage one to continue. Have FAITH in. The more I strengthen the Core of FAITH – Insight, the stronger my FAITH becomes. To the point it's on auto pilot and I'm at peace IN it.

Tad Deeper. The more I strengthen the Core of INSIGHT – Faith, the stronger my INSIGHT becomes. To the point it's on auto pilot and I'm at peace IN it.

2nd PERSEVERANCE: Requires ACCOUNTABILITY. Balancing. Follow Through. Harnessing One's Own Passion.

Tad Deeper. Accountability is the Core of Perseverance. Deeper. Perseverance is the Core of Accountability.

Thus, physical hearing. One must hear to understand at a deeper level; of what is balancing everything together, to persevere on. Being accountable to myself, allows myself to persevere. Thus, the fruits in Harnessing my passion, can be attained.

The more I strengthen the Core of PERSEVERANCE – Accountability, the stronger my PERSEVERANCE becomes. To the point it's on auto pilot and I'm at peace IN it.

Tad Deeper. The more I strengthen the Core of ACCOUNTABILITY – Perseverance, the stronger my ACCOUNTABILITY becomes. To the point it's on auto pilot and I'm at peace IN it.

3rd LOVE: Requires COMPASSION. Naturally putting others before oneself. The Greater Good of an Enriching Relationship, Family, Community.

Tad Deeper. Compassion is the Core of Love. Deeper. Love is the Core of Compassion.

Thus, physical taste. It is in the tasting of something new, that makes our journey that more enriching. Tasting enhances our experience in connecting with creation. The total experience; has a unique taste of its own, to the point I LOVE it.

The more I strengthen the Core of LOVE – Compassion, the stronger my LOVE becomes. To the point it's on auto pilot and I'm at peace IN it.

Tad Deeper. The more I strengthen the Core of COMPASSION – Love, the stronger my COMPASSION becomes. To the point it's on auto pilot and I'm at peace IN it.

4th EXTROVERT: Requires FORGIVENESS. Reaching Out Beyond. Comfortable with first time conversations, anyone, anywhere and anytime. Feels at peace when adventuring out, to connect with new people and creation.

Note: This characteristic can only be maximized with the commitment to one's spiritmate. Example: Without being maximized with a spiritmate, this characteristic goes to 75%. It will have the feeling of being 100% though. When one commits to their spiritmate they'll soon realize, dang "I got to go deeper in reaching out; to being vulnerable, forgiving and patient." Once mastered, looking back the individual will say, dang "My EXTROVERT wasn't 100%, when I thought it was."

Tad Deeper. Forgiveness is the Core of Being Extrovert. Deeper. Extrovert is the Core of Forgiveness.

Thus, physical touch. Touch is the greatest thing that the Unconditional Love part of the Spirit EVER Created. Period. It helps us see better when we can't see. Get an idea of what something might taste and smell like, before eating it. At sensitive moments; touch can speak more words, than we could ever dream to say. And respectful gentle touching; can make a relationship that much more deeper and enriching. Period 2.0

The more I strengthen the Core of EXTROVERT – Forgiveness, the stronger my EXTROVERT becomes. To the point it's on auto pilot and I'm at peace IN it.

Tad Deeper. The more I strengthen the Core of FORGIVENESS – Extrovert, the stronger my FORGIVENESS becomes. To the point it's on auto pilot and I'm at peace IN it.

Note 2.0 This is why this characteristic; is best understood, in my committed spiritmate relationship.

5th TEACHING: Requires PEACE. Explaining the Details in Easy Steps. One on One. Entire Group. Understands the Five Characteristics and Teaches Them Accordingly, from the Listener's Current Understanding.

Any Subject of Interest and the Mechanics of each. The Peace in Understanding what the subject is, and where the listener is at in the subject. Gently helps the listener where they are at in the subject, to the understanding of the subject completely. At their speed of comprehension. The teacher is so at peace in teaching; that they can teach one or a whole room full, at the same time. By customizing the teaching technique to the crowd size.

Tad Deeper. Peace is the Core of Teaching. Deeper. Teaching is the Core of Peace.

Thus, physical smell. Smell helps one to understand a situation better. Where to start and how to proceed. Smelling goes beyond aromas, to how creation is behaving. "That doesn't smell right." And how the individual creation is interacting with each other…

A classic is when caring parents, smell a poopy diaper. **Yup. I said it.** I can. I was a *single parent* father; of my three beautiful children, for 13+ years. AND with no help. I stayed single to invest all my unworking hours, into my children. Priceless. I would do it All Over again, without blinking an eye. Hmmm. *OV, stay focus here bro! Lol.*

The more I strengthen the Core of TEACHING – Peace, the stronger my TEACHING becomes. To the point it's on auto pilot and I'm at peace IN it.

Tad Deeper. The more I strengthen the Core of PEACE – Teaching, the stronger my PEACE becomes. To the point it's on auto pilot and I'm at peace IN it.

UNDERSTANDING THESE FIVE CHARACTERISTICS; ARE THE COMPONENTS, OF THE FIVE PHASES OF CREATION'S LIFE:

Reread that a few times.

Slowly…

Let it Absorb Deep into Your Core.

THE FIVE COMPONENTS OF EACH CHARACTERISTIC OF UNCONDITIONAL LOVE:

Note: These Five Components are the Same for Each Characteristic.

1ST CHILD: Learning How to Spiritually, Mentally and, Physically Connect with Creation.

Learning that Specific Characteristic from a Child's Perspective. **Phase One.**

2nd ADULT: Learning How to Spiritually, Mentally and Physically Maturely, Respectively and Responsibly Connect with Creation.

Learning that Specific Characteristic from an Adult's Perspective. **Phase Two.**

3rd FRIEND: Learning How to Embrace Each Other's Differences; while Enjoying Each Other's Company, Sharing Tasks Together, Solving Problems.

Learning that Specific Characteristic from a Friend's Perspective. **Phase Three.**

4th COMPANION: Learning How to Become a Companion in One Spirit, One Mind, One Body and Be at Peace with It; in Everything thing we do together, as Spiritmates.

Learning that Specific Characteristic from a Companion's Perspective. **Phase Four.** *Aka Final Phase.*

5th PARENT: Learning How to Spiritually, Mentally, and Physically Maturely Procreate; a Child and Nurture Them, with my Spiritmate.

Learning that Specific Characteristic from a Parent's Perspective. **Phase Five.**

The Parent Phase Brings All the Phases Full Circle. The Parent while interacting with their Child; will be a mirror reflection to them, on how they were as a child.

Each Phase of Physical Created Life; has All of the five characteristics, **within** that physical life experience…

Each of the Five Characteristics; has All of the five Physical Phases/Components of Creation's Life, within that characteristic.

All five experiences/phases must be physically lived through; to completely understand Unconditional Love part of the Spirit, to its **FULLEST.** And the meaning of these five words… FAITH, PERSERVANCE, COMPASSION, FORGIVENESS AND PEACE.

READ THIS SLOWLY. LET YOUR CORE ABSORB IT…

When I'm at TOTAL PEACE; with each characteristic of that phase, with all Five Phases. Then I will naturally be at TOTAL PEACE, with every aspect of my life…

If there is a Phase that I'm not at peace with; then I will always be struggling, with that area in my life…

Struggling Signs with Characteristics are: Panic, Anger, Revenge, Anxiety and Depression. Justifying my concerns, approaches and beliefs.

ALL FIVE CHARACTERISTICS are always operating in one's life.

Now Let's Go Deeper…

We all have a *minor* and *major* characteristic, that is predominate in our lives. The minor characteristic is what we speak with, ALL the time. The major characteristic is what we think of ALL the time; no matter what condition, and or season we are in. **PERIOD.**

Example: If my major is INSIGHT and my minor is ACCOUNTABILITY; then it's going to be easy for me, to relate to others with the same combo. *If the combo is opposite* then it will still be easy to work with; **but will need** to tweak our communication, from time to time. At "crunch" times it might get intense though.

Note: The Communication will be easy to tweak, because both can relate to each other's examples. Due to the same characteristic combos.

FOR SPIRITMATES TO MAXIMIZE getting along with each other; they will need to have the same, major and minor characteristics. No matter how they're feeling; going through and or season they're in, with their relationship. They will always easily understand and enjoy each other. It's like each other is reading, each other's minds.

Example: Their Majors are INSIGHT and their Minors are ACCOUNTABILITY.

NOTE: Odds are high that they *will be the same and or switched*. This will be confirmation to them, that they were together in the beginning. When the Unconditional Love part of the Spirit created them as a couple/companions.

Examples: Both Majors are INSIGHT and Minors are ACCOUNTABILITY. **OR** One's Major is INSIGHT and the Other's is ACCOUNTABILITY. ***Thus spiritmates.***

EXTRA NOTE: When both spiritmates have the same Majors and Minors. ***But*** their Majors and Minor's: Macros and Micros are switched; *it will be* **even easier** for them to tweak their understanding of each other.

Examples: Both Majors are INSIGHT and Minors are ACCOUNTABILITY. One's Major is Macro and the Other's is Micro.

One's Minor is Micro and the Other's is Macro. The tweaking will be **A LOT Easier.** Again at "crunch" times might not be.

The **EXTRA PLUS** is when they both mastering tweaking on autopilot, IT WILL ACTUALLY HONE Their Accomplishments A lot and Big Time. The Densities will be a whole lot stronger. As well as their satisfaction as spiritmates. This will be like tingling sensations on top of their goose bumps. Lol

To help dial in this understanding to the nth degree, these are the
macro and micro version to each characteristic:

INSIGHT is operating either in macro or micro.

Macro is overall "big picture" vision. **Example:** Sees the direction of the whole community.

Micro is seeing the finest details. **Example:** Sees why the community is heading in a direction.

ACCOUNTABILITY is operating in macro or micro.

Macro is overall understanding of completing a project. **Example:** Knows All the components to make a strong community.

Micro is understanding the specific details of the complete project. **Example**: Knows the specific details of each individual component, to make a strong community.

Note: This Characteristic contains All Five of the Characteristics in equal proportions. Example: 20% Insight + 20% Accountability + 20% Compassion + 20% Extrovert + 20% Teaching = 100% Accountability.

> ***Thus, the natural ability*** to balance everything at any time. At times they might be in different proportions. This allows for better needed communication between the macros and micros.

COMPASSION is operating in macro or micro.

Macro is overall compassion of the relationship, family, child, friend, stranger, etc. **Example:**

Orchestrating Family Get togethers, Doing Activities Together and Community Outreaches.

Micro is at the finest details of compassionately; connecting within the relationship, family, child, friend, stranger, etc. **Example:** Enriching One on One Family moments, doing one on one activities together and one on one community outreaches.

EXTROVERT is operating in macro or micro.

Macro is the overall reaching out to new: friendships, communities, neighbors, etc. **Example:** Being a part of an Overall Outreach Mentorship Community.

Micro is reaching out to new: friendships, communities, neighbors, etc. *uniquely* in deeper ways. **Example:** Reaches out to individuals; in helping them connect, to where they want to go next in their lives.

TEACHING is operating in macro or micro.

Macro is the overall helping those understand the five characteristics of Unconditional Love part of the Spirit, Concepts, Techniques, Etc. **Example:** Teaching Classroom to Auditorium Size Crowds.

Micro is helping those understand *the details* of the each of the five characteristics of the Unconditional Love part of the Spirit, Concepts, Techniques, Etc. **Example:** One on One teaching of specifics of skills, techniques and Concepts.

In Summary...

The Rosetta Stone of Unconditional Love helps me, locate these troubled areas in my life. As well as, in helping me restore my relationships.

It honestly assists me and my relationships to move forward together; in our lives and relationships, in spirit, mind and body.

The Rosetta Stone of Unconditional Love as a counselor, helps us to understand the words: FAITH, PRESERVERANCE, COMPASSION, FORGIVENESS AND PEACE. Through each of the Five Physical Phases we go through. While putting: panic, anger, revenge, anxiety and depression in their places.

AGAIN DISCLAIMER: The Rosetta Stone of Unconditional Love does not help self-centered love people. It might only reveal proof of self-centered love, by how the person reacts to specific questions.

If so; then might be best to stop the session, and or skip over to avoid conflicts.

The CHARACTERISTICS OF UNCONDITIONAL LOVE

In a Table Graft Nutshell. *Oops. Stay Focused OV*. As Referenced in ETERNALING

CREATION Final Phase, Author Optimum Vizhan. 2024.

| THE SPIRIT: When Creating Friends || ||
| 50% Unconditional Love || 50% Self-Centered Love ||
5 CHARACTERISTICS	CORE:	5 CHARACTERISTICS	CORE:
Eyes: Insight	Faith	Nosight	Panic
Hearing: Accountability	Perseverance	Uncommitted	Anger
Taste: Love	Compassion	Hatred	Revenge
Touch: Extrovert	Forgiveness	Introvert	Anxiety
Smell: Teaching	Peace	Doubt	Depression
NOTE: The Core of Faith is Insight, The Core of Perseverance is Accountably, The Core of Compassion is Love, The Core of Forgiveness is Extrovert, The Core of Peace is Teaching.		**NOTE:** The Core of Panic is Nosight, The Core of Anger is Uncommitted, The Core of Revenge is Hatred, The Core of Anxiety is Introvert, The Core of Depression is Doubt.	

READ THIS SLOW AND LET YOUR CORE ABSORB THIS...

Note: At First this might sound like a repeat. It's just explaining all this; in another way to help us, who might be feeling overwhelmed right now.

The Core of FAITH is INSIGHT. Insight Sees the total purpose and the necessary critical details. Faith produces Insight.

When we embrace faith; especially when we don't want to, that faith will strengthen our Insight even deeper. At first, we might struggle. But we need to keep pressing forward to prime the well. Once the well of Faith is primed; it will automatically produce INSIGHT, when we need it. Wow that was deep. Pardon the Pun. *Was that Punny?*

The Core of PERSEVERANCE is ACCOUNTABILITY. Accountability balances all five characteristics out. Perseverance produces Accountability.

When we embrace perseverance; especially when we don't want to, that perseverance will strengthen our Accountability even deeper. At first, we might struggle. But we need to keep pressing forward to prime the well. Once the well of Perseverance is primed; it will automatically produce ACCOUNTABILITY when we need it. Wow that was deep. Pardon the Pun. *Was that Punny 2.0?*

The Core of COMPASSION Is LOVE. Love has Compassion for and with All of Creation. Compassion produces Love.

When we embrace compassion; especially when we don't want to, that compassion will strengthen our Love even deeper. At first, we might struggle. But we need to keep pressing forward to prime the well. Once the well of Compassion is primed; it will automatically produce LOVE when we need it. Wow that was deep. Pardon the Pun. *Was that Punny 3.0?*

The Core of Forgiveness is EXTROVERT. Extrovert reaches out to All of Creation, to create new enriching two-way friendships. Forgiveness produces being an Extrovert.

When we embrace forgiveness; especially when we don't want to, that forgiveness will strengthen our Extrovert even deeper. At first, we might struggle. But we need to keep pressing forward to prime the well. Once the well of Forgiveness is primed; it will automatically produce EXTROVERT when we need it. Wow that was deep. Pardon the Pun. *Was that Punny 4.0?*

The Core of Peace is TEACHING. Teaching to understand each of the five characteristics, relationships and creation. Concepts, Techniques, Etc. Peace produces Teaching.

When we embrace peace; especially when we don't want to, that peace will strengthen our Teaching even deeper. At first, we might struggle. But we need to keep pressing forward to prime the well. Once the well of Peace is primed; it will automatically produce TEACHING when we need it. Wow that was deep. Pardon the Pun. *Was that Punny 5.0?*

Ok bro, we need to take a break OV.

Ok. Break Time. I was about to fall asleep – it's like 2am. *Perfect Timing.*

Components of the Five Words:

Faith: Child, Sight, Visionary.
Perseverance: Adult, Hearing, Accountable.
Compassion: Friend, Taste, Assistant.
Forgiveness: Companion, Touch, ProCreators.
Peace: Parent, Smell, Mentor.

Then After Phase Four. Entering Phase Five:

As Referenced in ETERNALING CREATION Final Phase,

Author Optimum Vizhan. 2024.

THE SPIRIT:	
With Friends Physically Eternal	
100% Unconditional Love	
5 CHARACTERISTICS	CORE:
Insight	Faith
Accountability	Perseverance
Love	Compassion
Extrovert	Forgiveness
Teaching	Peace
NOTE: The Core of Faith is Insight, The Core of Perseverance is Accountably, The Core of Compassion is Love, The Core of Forgiveness is Extrovert, The Core of Peace is Teaching.	

Now Without Further Due

Here is…

THE ROSETTA STONE OF UNCONDITIONAL LOVE FUNDAMENTAL COMPONENTS FOR ONE PERSON.

CHILD
PHASE ONE
EYES
INSIGHT

👁 ○
👂 ○
😋 ○
👆 ○
👃 ○
PEACE ○

ADULT
PHASE TWO
HEARING
ACCOUNTABLITY

👁 ○
👂 ○
😋 ○
👆 ○
👃 ○
PEACE ○

FRIEND
PHASE THREE
TASTE
UNCONDITIONAL LOVE

👁 ○
👂 ○
😋 ○
👆 ○
👃 ○
PEACE ○

COMPANION
PHASE FOUR
TOUCH
EXTROVERT

👁 ○
👂 ○
😋 ○
👆 ○
👃 ○
PEACE ○

PARENT
PHASE FIVE
SMELL
TEACHING

👁 ○
👂 ○
😋 ○
👆 ○
👃 ○
PEACE ○

the ROSETTA STONE of UNCONDITIONAL LOVE
Author: Optimum Vizhan. Copyright 2024.

WHEN 100% INMERSED IN THE UNCONDITIONAL LOVE PART OF THE SPIRIT; NOTHING WILL SEPARATE US EVER AGAIN. NEVER EVER, EVER AGAIN. PERIOD. Take a bath in that, and let it soak in.

In this Section; we get introduced to the Rosetta Stone of Unconditional Love Diagram, looking at it as one person. This is a blown-up view of the one person. So that we can slowly; absorb the understanding, of this Rosetta Stone of Unconditional Love Diagram.

We also get introduced to the questions I ask myself; to determine if I'm at peace with that specific characteristic, while going through that phase of my eternal life.

For convenience we will break this down by each phase; so that we don't have to keep flipping through the pages, to color in the empty circles.

READY? LET'S GO...

CHILD PHASE ONE EYES INSIGHT 👁 ○ 👂 ○ 👅 ○ 👆 ○ 👃 ○ PEACE ○

the ROSETTA STONE of UNCONDITIONAL LOVE
Author: Optimum Vizhan. Copyright 2024.

We put these in the horizontal position, to take less space. So; we can reference to it close by, versus flipping through a bunch of pages.

The first component; of each characteristic is Going Through, is the Child Phase. Labeled as PHASE ONE.

As a CHILD, I'm Learning How to Spiritually, Mentally and, Physically Connect with Creation.

FAITH: Requires INSIGHT. I'm Seeing the Physical Insights of Doing Something *without any prior physical* knowledge and training. **Note:** Read ETERNALIZING CREATION Final Phase, to fully understand and appreciate this phase.

During My Child Phase; I need to learn how to be at peace with each characteristic, from My **Child's Perspective.**

When we know; we are at peace with that characteristic, we color in the circle next to the icon. Icons are: the eye for insight, ear for hearing, face with tongue for taste, hand with pointing finger for touch and nose for smell.

OK. LET'S START WITH THE QUESTIONS...

EYE: INSIGHT, FAITH, VISIONARY

1. **Do I See Life at a Deeper Level?**
2. When I See Something I Like, Do I Try it Myself?
3. When I See Someone Hurting, Do I Try to Help Them?
4. I Got to See the Next New Thing Now.
5. Do I Like Showing People What I Learned?

1. **Do I Believe Strongly in Something?**
2. When I See Someone Doing Something, Do I Try it Myself?
3. When I See Something Not Safe, Do I Tell Someone?
4. I like Showing People the Next New Thing.
5. Do I Reassure Loved Ones and Others It Will Be Ok?

BONUS QUESTION: Do I Enjoy Looking at All Types of Creation, through My Child Perspective?

HEARING: ACCOUNTABILITY, PERSEVERANCE

1. **Do I Hear Life at a Deeper Level?**
2. Do I Listen on How to Put Things Together – Easily?
3. When I Hear Someone Hurting, Do I Try to Help Them?
4. Do I Forgive People Easily, When They Talk to Me?
5. Do I Like to Listen, to People Trying to Teach Me Something?

1. **Do I Listen to New Ideas with Enthusiasm?**
2. If I Hear Something I Like, Do I Do It Myself?
3. When I Hear Something Not Safe, Do I Tell Someone?
4. When I Do Something Wrong, Do I Say Sorry Upfront?
5. Do I Teach Others What I Heard About Earlier?

BONUS QUESTION: Do I Enjoy Hearing All Types of Sounds, through My Child Perspective?

TASTE: LOVE, COMPASSION, ASSISTANT

1. **Do I Love Life at a Deeper Level?**
2. Do I Love How to Put Things Together – Easily?
3. When I Assist Someone Who is Hurting, Do I Try Hard to Help Them?
4. Do I Assist People Easily?
5. Do I Like Teaching People While Assisting Them?

1. **Am I Strongly Compassionate in Something?**
2. If I Love Something I Like, do I Do It Myself?
3. When I Experience Something Not Safe, Do I Tell Someone?
4. I Love Being Assistants with Others. Especially New People?
5. I Love Teaching People, Who Want to Learn How to Assist Others.

BONUS QUESTION: Do I Enjoy Tasting Things; to See How They Taste, through My Child Perspective?

TOUCH: EXTROVERT, FORGIVENESS

1. **Do I Forgive Life at a Deeper Level?**
2. Do I Reach Out to Put Things Together – Easily?
3. When I Feel Someone Hurting, Do I Try to Help Them?
4. Do I Reach Out to Forgive "Strangers" Easily?
5. Do I Love Teaching Hands on with People, What I Learned?

1. **Do I See Creation's Relationships Being Restored?**
2. I Know Many Tangible Ways to Reach Out to People?
3. Enriching Relationships is a High Priority?
4. I Show My Love to People Through My Actions?
5. I Love Teaching People, How to Work with Their Hands?

BONUS QUESTION: Do I Enjoy Touching Things to See How They Feel, through My Child Perspective?

SMELL: TEACHING, PEACE

1. Do I Smell Life at a Deeper Level?
2. Am I Totally at Peace Putting Things Together?
3. Do I Peacefully Help Those Who Need It?
4. Do I Go Great Distances in Making People Feel Safe?
5. Am I Peacefully Teaching People How to Be Peaceful?

1. Do I Believe Strongly in Teaching Peace to Everyone?
2. I Understand Why Things Smell the Way They Do?
3. When Someone is Panicking, I Comfort Them with Peace?
4. When I Smell Something Wrong, Do I Say Something Upfront?
5. I Can Teach Any Subject Peaceably, in Any Circumstance?

BONUS QUESTION: Do I Seek All Types of Smells that Make Me Feel Peaceful, through My Child Perspective?

These Questions are to Help Us Search within Our Childhood Experiences, and be convinced I'm at peace with my childhood.

In my Child like way, I embraced my experiences as ways of learning these characteristics.

If I'm at 100% peace with learning that specific characteristic, then I fill that associated empty circle in.

Note: If not quite sure; then leave the circle empty and go onto the next characteristic, in this child phase.

When I have filled in all the characteristics circles. And convinced of being totally at peace; with my childhood learning experiences, then fill in the peace empty circle.

Congratulations! Either way. We are Embracing Our Unconditional Love Friendship Journey with ourselves, our loved ones and the Unconditional Love part of the Spirit.

ADULT PHASE TWO HEARING ACTABLY 👁 O 👂 O 😋 O ☝ O 👃 O PEACE O

the ROSETTA STONE of UNCONDITIONAL LOVE
Author: Optimum Vizhan. Copyright 2024.

The Second Component; of each characteristic is Going Through, is the Adult Phase. Labeled as PHASE TWO.

As an ADULT, I'm Learning How to Spiritually, Mentally and Physically Maturely, Respectively and Responsibly Connect with Creation.

PERSEVERANCE: Requires ACCOUNTABILITY. I'm Balancing. I'm Following Through. I'm

Harnessing My Own Passion.

During My Adult Phase; I need to learn how to be peace with each characteristic, from My **Adult's Perspective**.

When we know; we are at peace with that characteristic, we color in the circle next to the icon. Icons are: the eye for insight, ear for hearing, face with tongue for taste, hand with pointing finger for touch and nose for smell.

OK. LET'S START WITH THE QUESTIONS…

EYE: INSIGHT, FAITH, VISIONARY

1. **Do I See Life at a Deeper Level?**
2. When I See Something I Like, Do I Try it Myself?
3. When I See Someone Hurting, Do I Try to Help Them?
4. I Got to See the Next New Thing Now.
5. Do I Like Showing People What I Learned?

1. **Do I Believe Strongly in Something?**
2. When I See Someone Doing Something, Do I Try it Myself?
3. When I See Something Not Safe, Do I Tell Someone?
4. I like Showing People the Next New Thing.
5. Do I Reassure Loved Ones and Others It Will Be Ok?

BONUS QUESTION: Do I Enjoy Looking at All Types of Creation, through My Adult Perspective?

HEARING: ACCOUNTABILITY, PERSEVERANCE

1. **Do I Hear Life at a Deeper Level?**
2. Do I Listen on How to Put Things Together – Easily?
3. When I Hear Someone Hurting, Do I Try to Help Them?
4. Do I Forgive People Easily When They Talk to Me?
5. Do I Like to Listen, to People Trying to Teach Me Something?

1. **Do I Listen to New Ideas with Enthusiasm?**
2. If I Hear Something I Like, Do I Do It Myself?
3. When I Hear Something Not Safe, Do I Tell Someone?
4. When I Do Something Wrong, Do I Say Sorry Upfront?
5. Do I Teach Others What I Heard About Earlier?

BONUS QUESTION: Do I Enjoy Hearing All Types of Sounds, through My Adult Perspective?

TASTE: LOVE, COMPASSION, ASSISTANT

1. **Do I Love Life at a Deeper Level?**

2. Do I Love How to Put Things Together – Easily?
   3. When I Assist Someone that is Hurting, Do I Try Hard to Help Them?
   4. Do I Assist People Easily?
   5. Do I Like Teaching People While Assisting Them?

   1. Am I Strongly Compassionate in Something?
   2. If I Love Something I Like, Do I Do It Myself?
   3. When I Experience Something Not Safe, Do I Tell Someone?
   4. I Love Being Assistants with Others. Especially New People?
   5. I Love Teaching People, Who Want to Learn How to Assist Others.

BONUS QUESTION: Do I Enjoy Tasting Things to See How They Taste, through My Adult Perspective?

TOUCH: EXTROVERT, FORGIVENESS

   1. Do I Forgive Life at a Deeper Level?
   2. Do I Reach Out to Put Things Together – Easily?
   3. When I Feel Someone, Hurting Do I Try to Help Them?
   4. Do I Reach Out to Forgive "Strangers" Easily?
   5. Do I Love Teaching Hands on with People, What I Learned?

   1. Do I See Creation's Relationships Being Restored?
   2. I Know Many Tangible Ways to Reach Out to People?
   3. Enriching Relationships is a High Priority?
   4. I Show My Love to People Through My Actions?
   5. I Love Teaching People, How to Work with Their Hands?

BONUS QUESTION: Do I Enjoy Touching Things to See How They Feel, through My Adult Perspective?

SMELL: TEACHING, PEACE

   1. Do I Smell Life at a Deeper Level?
   2. Am I Totally at Peace Putting Things Together?
   3. Do I Peacefully Help Those Who Need It?
   4. Do I Go Great Distances in Making People Feel Safe?
   5. Am I Peacefully Teaching People How to Be Peaceful?

   1. Do I Believe Strongly in Teaching Peace to Everyone?
   2. I Understand Why Things Smell the Way They Do?
   3. When Someone is Panicking, I Comfort Them with Peace?
   4. When I Smell Something Wrong, Do I Say Something Upfront?
   5. I Can Teach Any Subject Peaceably, in Any Circumstance?

BONUS QUESTION: Do I Seek All Types of Smells that Make Me Feel Peaceful, through My Adult Perspective?

These Questions are to Help Us Search within Our Adult Experiences, and be convinced I'm at peace with my Adult Life.

In my Adult like way, I embraced my experiences as ways of learning these characteristics.

If I'm at 100% peace with learning that specific characteristic, then I fill that associated empty circle in.

Note: If not quite sure, then leave the circle empty and go onto the next characteristic in this child phase.

When I have filled in all the characteristics circles; and convince of being totally at peace with my adult learning experiences, then fill in the peace empty circle.

Congratulations! Either way. We are Embracing Our Unconditional Love Friendship Journey with ourselves, our loved ones and the Unconditional Love part of the Spirit.

FRIEND PHASE THREE TASTE LOVE O O O O O PEACE O

the ROSETTA STONE of UNCONDITIONAL LOVE
Author: Optimum Vizhan. Copyright 2024.

The Third Component; of each characteristic is Going Through, is the Friend Phase. Labeled as PHASE THREE.

As a FRIEND, I'm Learning How to Embrace Our Differences; while Enjoying Each Other's Company, Sharing Tasks Together, Solving Problems.

LOVE: Requires COMPASSION. I'm Naturally putting others before myself. For the Greater Good of my Enriching Relationships, My Family, My Community.

During My Friend Phase; I need to learn how to be peace with each characteristic, from My Being a **Friend's Perspective.**

When we know; we are at peace with that characteristic, we color in the circle next to the icon. Icons are: the eye for insight, ear for hearing, face with tongue for taste, hand with pointing finger for touch and nose for smell.

OK. LET'S START WITH THE QUESTIONS…

EYE: INSIGHT, FAITH, VISIONARY

    1. **Do I See Life at a Deeper Level?**
    2. When I See Something I Like, Do I Try it Myself?
    3. When I See Someone Hurting, Do I Try to Help Them?

4. I Got to See the Next New Thing Now.
   5. Do I Like Showing People What I Learned?

   1. Do I Believe Strongly in Something?
   2. When I See Someone Doing Something, Do I Try it Myself?
   3. When I See Something Not Safe, Do I Tell Someone?
   4. I like Showing People the Next New Thing.
   5. Do I Reassure Loved Ones and Others It Will Be Ok?

BONUS QUESTION: Do I Enjoy Looking at All Types of Creation, through My Being a Friend Perspective?

HEARING: ACCOUNTABILITY, PERSEVERANCE

   1. Do I Hear Life at a Deeper Level?
   2. Do I Listen on How to Put Things Together – Easily?
   3. When I Hear Someone Hurting, Do I Try to Help Them?
   4. Do I Forgive People Easily When They Talk to Me?
   5. Do I Like to Listen, to People Trying to Teach Me Something?

   1. Do I Listen to New Ideas with Enthusiasm?
   2. If I Hear Something I Like, Do I Do It Myself?
   3. When I Hear Something Not Safe, Do I Tell Someone?
   4. When I Do Something Wrong, Do I Say Sorry Upfront?
   5. Do I Teach Others What I Heard About Earlier?

BONUS QUESTION: Do I Enjoy Hearing All Types of Sounds, through My Being a Friend Perspective?

TASTE: LOVE, COMPASSION, ASSISTANT

   1. Do I Love Life at a Deeper Level?
   2. Do I Love How to Put Things Together – Easily?
   3. When I Assist Someone that is Hurting, Do I Try Hard to Help Them?
   4. Do I Assist People Easily?
   5. Do I Like Teaching People While Assisting Them?

   1. Am I Strongly Compassionate in Something?
   2. If I Love Something I Like, Do I Do It Myself?
   3. When I Experience Something Not Safe, Do I Tell Someone?
   4. I Love Being Assistants with Others. Especially New People?
   5. I Love Teaching People, Who Want to Learn How to Assist Others.

BONUS QUESTION: Do I Enjoy Tasting Things to See How They Taste, through My Being a Friend Perspective?

TOUCH: EXTROVERT, FORGIVENESS

1. **Do I Forgive Life at a Deeper Level?**
2. Do I Reach Out to Put Things Together – Easily?
3. When I Feel Someone, Hurting Do I Try to Help Them?
4. Do I Reach Out to Forgive "Strangers" Easily?
5. Do I Love Teaching Hands on with People, What I Learned?

1. **Do I See Creation's Relationships Being Restored?**
2. I Know Many Tangible Ways to Reach Out to People?
3. Enriching Relationships is a High Priority?
4. I Show My Love to People Through My Actions?
5. I Love Teaching People, How to Work with Their Hands?

BONUS QUESTION: Do I Enjoy Touching Things to See How They Feel, through My Being a Friend Perspective?

SMELL: TEACHING, PEACE

1. **Do I Smell Life at a Deeper Level?**
2. Am I Totally at Peace Putting Things Together?
3. Do I Peacefully Help Those Who Need It?
4. Do I Go Great Distances in Making People Feel Safe?
5. Am I Peacefully Teaching People How to Be Peaceful?

1. **Do I Believe Strongly in Teaching Peace to Everyone?**
2. I Understand Why Things Smell the Way They Do?
3. When Someone is Panicking, I Comfort Them with Peace?
4. When I Smell Something Wrong, Do I Say Something Upfront?
5. I Can Teach Any Subject Peaceably, in Any Circumstance?

BONUS QUESTION: Do I Seek All Types of Smells that Make Me Feel Peaceful, through My Being a Friend Perspective?

These Questions are to Help Us Search within Our Being a Friend Experiences, and be convinced I'm at peace with my Being a Friend.

In my Friend like way, I embraced my experiences as ways of learning these characteristics.

If I'm at 100% peace with learning that specific characteristic, then I fill that associated empty circle in.

Note: If not quite sure, then leave the circle empty and go onto the next characteristic in this Being a Friend phase.

When I have filled in all the characteristics circles, and convince of being totally at peace with my Friendship learning experiences then fill in the peace empty circle.

Congratulations! Either way. We are Embracing Our Unconditional Love Friendship Journey with ourselves, our loved ones and the Unconditional Love part of the Spirit.

OPTIMUM VIZHAN

COMPANION   PHASE FOUR TOUCH   EXTROVERT   👁 ⭕ 👂 ⭕ 👅 ⭕ 👆 ⭕ 👃 ⭕ PEACE ⭕

the ROSETTA STONE of UNCONDITIONAL LOVE
Author: Optimum Vizhan. Copyright 2024.

The Fourth Component; of each characteristic is Going Through, is the Companion's Phase. Labeled as PHASE FOUR. *Aka Final Phase.*

As a COMPANION, I'm Learning How to Become a Companion in One Spirit, One Mind, One Body and Be at Peace with It; in Everything thing we do together, as Spiritmates.

EXTROVERT: Requires FORGIVENESS. Reaching Out Beyond Myself. Comfortable with first time conversations, anyone, anywhere and anytime. I Feel at peace when adventuring out, to connect with new people and creation. Especially with my spiritmate. I will need to be completely open; to all aspects of my physical life, with my spiritmate. This will allow me to come at peace with this characteristic.

During My Companion Phase; I need to learn how to be peace with each characteristic, from My Being a **Companion's Perspective.**

When we know; we are at peace with that characteristic, we color in the circle next to the icon. Icons are: the eye for insight, ear for hearing, face with tongue for taste, hand with pointing finger for touch and nose for smell.

OK. LET'S START WITH THE QUESTIONS…

EYE: INSIGHT, FAITH, VISIONARY

    1. **Do I See Life at a Deeper Level?**
    2. When I See Something I Like, Do I Try it Myself?
    3. When I See Someone Hurting, Do I Try to Help Them?
    4. I Got to See the Next New Thing Now.
    5. Do I Like Showing People What I Learned?

    1. **Do I Believe Strongly in Something?**
    2. When I See Someone Doing Something, Do I Try it Myself?
    3. When I See Something Not Safe, Do I Tell Someone?
    4. I like Showing People the Next New Thing.
    5. Do I Reassure Loved Ones and Others It Will Be Ok?

BONUS QUESTION: Do I Enjoy Looking at All Types of Creation, through My Companion Perspective?

HEARING: ACCOUNTABILITY, PERSEVERANCE

    1. Do I Hear Life at a Deeper Level?

2. Do I Listen on How to Put Things Together – Easily?
3. When I Hear Someone Hurting, Do I Try to Help Them?
4. Do I Forgive People Easily When They Talk to Me?
5. Do I Like to Listen, to People Trying to Teach Me Something?

1. **Do I Listen to New Ideas with Enthusiasm?**
2. If I Hear Something I Like, Do I Do It Myself?
3. When I Hear Something Not Safe, Do I Tell Someone?
4. When I Do Something Wrong, Do I Say Sorry Upfront?
5. Do I Teach Others What I Heard About Earlier?

BONUS QUESTION: Do I Enjoy Hearing All Types of Sounds, through My Companion Perspective?

TASTE: LOVE, COMPASSION, ASSISTANT

1. **Do I Love Life at a Deeper Level?**
2. Do I Love How to Put Things Together – Easily?
3. When I Assist Someone that is Hurting, Do I Try Hard to Help Them?
4. Do I Assist People Easily?
5. Do I Like Teaching People While Assisting Them?

1. **Am I Strongly Compassionate in Something?**
2. If I Love Something I Like, Do I Do It Myself?
3. When I Experience Something Not Safe, Do I Tell Someone?
4. I Love Being Assistants with Others. Especially New People?
5. I Love Teaching People, Who Want to Learn How to Assist Others.

BONUS QUESTION: Do I Enjoy Tasting Things to See How They Taste, through My Companion Perspective?

TOUCH: EXTROVERT, FORGIVENESS

1. **Do I Forgive Life at a Deeper Level?**
2. Do I Reach Out to Put Things Together – Easily?
3. When I Feel Someone, Hurting Do I Try to Help Them?
4. Do I Reach Out to Forgive "Strangers" Easily?
5. Do I Love Teaching Hands on with People, What I Learned?

1. **Do I See Creation's Relationships Being Restored?**
2. I Know Many Tangible Ways to Reach Out to People?
3. Enriching Relationships is a High Priority?
4. I Show My Love to People Through My Actions?
5. I Love Teaching People How, to Work with Their Hands?

BONUS QUESTION: Do I Enjoy Touching Things to See How They Feel, through My Companion Perspective?

SMELL: TEACHING, PEACE

1. Do I Smell Life at a Deeper Level?
2. Am I Totally at Peace Putting Things Together?
3. Do I Peacefully Help Those Who Need It?
4. Do I Go Great Distances in Making People Feel Safe?
5. Am I Peacefully Teaching People How to Be Peaceful?

1. Do I Believe Strongly in Teaching Peace to Everyone?
2. I Understand Why Things Smell the Way They Do?
3. When Someone is Panicking, I Comfort Them with Peace?
4. When I Smell Something Wrong, Do I Say Something Upfront?
5. I Can Teach Any Subject Peaceably, in Any Circumstance?

BONUS QUESTION: Do I Seek All Types of Smells that Make Me Feel Peaceful, through My Companion Perspective?

These Questions are to Help Us Search within Our Companion Experiences, and be convinced I'm at peace with my Being a Companion.

In my Companion like way, I embraced my experiences as ways of learning these characteristics.

If I'm at 100% peace with learning that specific characteristic, then I fill that associated empty circle in.

Note: If not quite sure, then leave the circle empty and go onto the next characteristic in this companion phase.

When I have filled in all the characteristics circles, and convince of being totally at peace with my companion learning experiences then fill in the peace empty circle.

Congratulations! Either way. We are Embracing Our Unconditional Love Friendship Journey with ourselves, our loved ones and the Unconditional Love part of the Spirit.

PARENT PHASE FIVE SMELL TEACHING

the ROSETTA STONE of UNCONDITIONAL LOVE
Author: Optimum Vizhan. Copyright 2024.

The Fifth Component; of each characteristic is Going Through, is the Parent's Phase. Labeled as PHASE FIVE.

As a PARENT, I'm Learning How to Spiritually, Mentally, and Physically Maturely Procreate; a Child and Nurture Them, with my Spiritmate.

TEACHING: Requires PEACE. Explaining the Details in Easy Steps to Our Child/ren. So that they can start to Understands the Five Characteristics from their Child's Perspective. Knowing the Child's Major and Minor Characteristics; will make it easier in Teaching Them Accordingly, from the Child's Current Understanding.

During My Parent Phase; I need to learn how to be peace with each characteristic, from My Being a **Parent's Perspective.**

The Parent Phase brings all the phases full circle. Thus, completing and being at peace with Unconditional Love. And the understanding of the meaning of the Five Words: FAITH, PERSEVERANCE, COMPASSION, FORGIVENESS and PEACE.

When we know; we are at peace with that characteristic, we color in the circle next to the icon. Icons are: the eye for insight, ear for hearing, face with tongue for taste, hand with pointing finger for touch and nose for smell.

OK. LET'S START WITH THE QUESTIONS…

EYE: INSIGHT, FAITH, VISIONARY

1. **Do I See Life at a Deeper Level?**
2. When I See Something I Like, Do I Try it Myself?
3. When I See Someone Hurting, Do I Try to Help Them?
4. I Got to See the Next New Thing Now.
5. Do I Like Showing People What I Learned?

1. **Do I Believe Strongly in Something?**
2. When I See Someone Doing Something, Do I Try it Myself?
3. When I See Something Not Safe, Do I Tell Someone?
4. I like Showing People the Next New Thing.
5. Do I Reassure Loved Ones and Others It Will Be Ok?

BONUS QUESTION: Do I Enjoy Looking at All Types of Creation, through My Parent Perspective?

HEARING: ACCOUNTABILITY, PERSEVERANCE

1. **Do I Hear Life at a Deeper Level?**
2. Do I Listen on How to Put Things Together – Easily?
3. When I Hear Someone Hurting, Do I Try to Help Them?
4. Do I Forgive People Easily When They Talk to Me?
5. Do I Like to Listen, to People Trying to Teach Me Something?

1. **Do I Listen to New Ideas with Enthusiasm?**
2. If I Hear Something I Like, Do I Do It Myself?
3. When I Hear Something Not Safe, Do I Tell Someone?
4. When I Do Something Wrong, Do I Say Sorry Upfront?
5. Do I Like to Listen, to People Trying to Teach Me Something?

BONUS QUESTION: Do I Enjoy Hearing All Types of Sounds, through My Parent Perspective?

TASTE: LOVE, COMPASSION, ASSISTANT
   1. **Do I Love Life at a Deeper Level?**
   2. Do I Love How to Put Things Together – Easily?
   3. When I Assist Someone that is Hurting, Do I Try Hard to Help Them?
   4. Do I Assist People Easily?
   5. Do I Like Teaching People While Assisting Them?

   1. **Am I Strongly Compassionate in Something?**
   2. If I Love Something I Like, Do I Do It Myself?
   3. When I Experience Something Not Safe, Do I Tell Someone?
   4. I Love Being Assistants with Others. Especially New People?
   5. I Love Teaching People, Who Want to Learn How to Assist Others.

BONUS QUESTION: Do I Enjoy Tasting Things to See How They Taste, through My Parent Perspective?

TOUCH: EXTROVERT, FORGIVENESS
   1. **Do I Forgive Life at a Deeper Level?**
   2. Do I Reach Out to Put Things Together – Easily?
   3. When I Feel Someone, Hurting Do I Try to Help Them?
   4. Do I Reach Out to Forgive "Strangers" Easily?
   5. Do I Love Teaching Hands on with People, What I Learned?

   1. **Do I See Creation's Relationships Being Restored?**
   2. I Know Many Tangible Ways to Reach Out to People?
   3. Enriching Relationships is a High Priority?
   4. I Show My Love to People Through My Actions?
   5. I Love Teaching People, How to Work with Their Hands?

BONUS QUESTION: Do I Enjoy Touching Things to See How They Feel, through My Parent Perspective?

SMELL: TEACHING, PEACE
   1. **Do I Smell Life at a Deeper Level?**
   2. Am I Totally at Peace Putting Things Together?
   3. Do I Peacefully Help Those Who Need It?
   4. Do I Go Great Distances in Making People Feel Safe?
   5. Am I Peacefully Teaching People How to Be Peaceful?

   1. **Do I Believe Strongly in Teaching Peace to Everyone?**
   2. I Understand Why Things Smell the Way They Do?

3. When Someone is Panicking, I Comfort Them with Peace?
4. When I Smell Something Wrong, Do I Say Something Upfront?
5. I Can Teach Any Subject Peaceably, in Any Circumstance

BONUS QUESTION: Do I Seek All Types of Smells that Make Me Feel Peaceful, through My Parent Perspective?

These Questions are to Help Us Search within Our Parent Experiences, and be convinced I'm at peace with my Being a Parent.

In my Parent like way, I embraced my experiences as ways of learning these characteristics.

If I'm at 100% peace with learning that specific characteristic, then I fill that associated empty circle in.

Note: If not quite sure, then leave the circle empty and go onto the next characteristic in this parent phase.

When I have filled in all the characteristics circles, and convince of being totally at peace with my parent learning experiences then fill in the peace empty circle.

Congratulations! Either way. We are Embracing Our Unconditional Love Friendship Journey with ourselves, our loved ones and the Unconditional Love part of the Spirit.

THE ROSETTA STONE OF UNCONDITIONAL LOVE FUNDAMENTAL COMPONENTS FOR UP TO FIVE PEOPLE

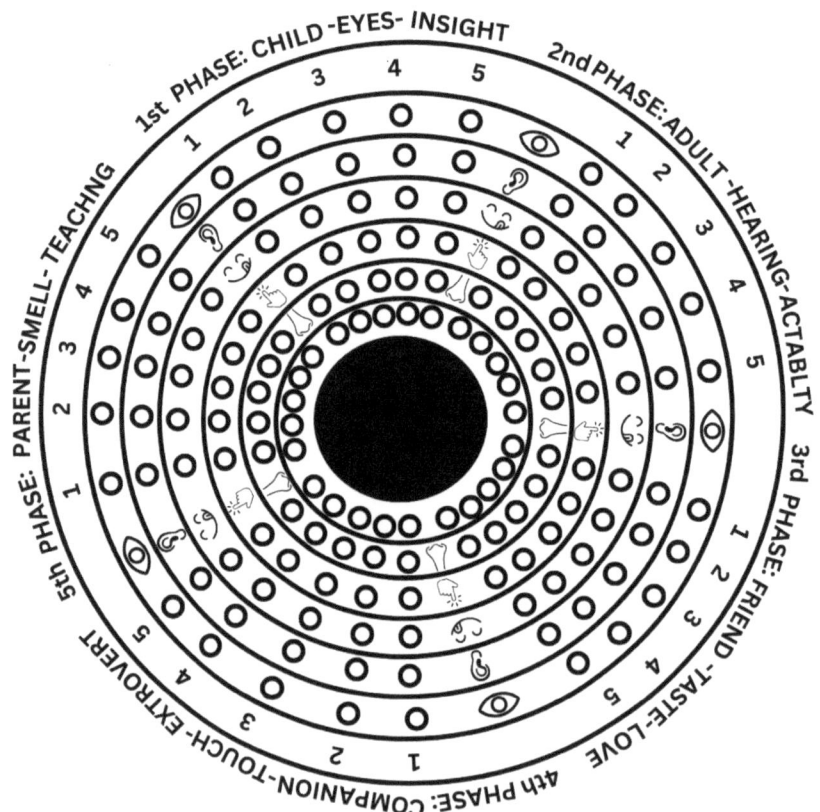

the ROSETTA STONE of UNCONDITIONAL LOVE
Author: Optimum Vizhan. Copyright 2024.

This Diagram is Great for Using with Groups Up to 5 People. The Group can see each other's progress and how to grow together in it.

This Diagram is Great for Couple's with up to Three Children as a Family. Assisting the Family into Learning Quicker; How to Communicate and Interact, with Each Other Better.

And or for Couple's Planning to have Children in the Near Future.

The **BLACK DOT** in the Middle Reminds Us to Clear Our Busy thoughts. And focus deeply on our personal reactions to the opportunities; challenges and successes we've had in each of the five phases, of our physical lives.

While Embracing Our Unconditional Love Journey Together.

HOW TO DISCOVER MY TWO DOMINATE CHARACTERISTICS

Now that we got a better understanding of what the five characteristics, components and phases of Unconditional Love and Creation. It will be easier to discover our two dominate characteristics.

Some of us, might have already figured out what two they are.

Either way, this Section will Help Determine for sure without a shadow of doubt.

We'll be Answering five questions, for each characteristic. The Questions will be written as statements, as though I am naturally thinking it.

If you purchase the paper back version of this book; then check off the statement/questions, when they apply/relate to you. Even if they are somewhat close.

The Top Two Characteristics; with the most check marks, are more than likely your two main characteristics.

If somewhat still fussy to you, then take a break. Pay Attention; closer to yourself how you're acting and commenting to those around you. This will help you, hone into your two main characteristics better.

In time with more encounters, challenges and "tense" situations; you'll be more convinced, these are you two main characteristics. Even test your possible two main characteristics; in these types of circumstances, to get more validation they are. NOTE: DO THIS RESPECTIVELY, GENTLY and CAUTIOSLY.

___ **INSIGHT:**

___ I Have Great Ideas that Are Not Currently Visible to the Masses.

It Makes Me Drool. lol

___ I Can See the Problems Others Can't See.

___ I Can See People's Passions and Unique Abilities.

___ I Can See the Best Way to Connect Groups, Networks and Solutions.

___ I Can See the Best Way to Teach People What They Want to Learn.

___ **ACCOUNTABILITY:**

___ I can See How to Solve Every Problem Before They are Problems.

          It Makes Me Drool. lol
___ I'm Making Sure All the Bases are Covered in All Situations.
___ I'm Doing Projects for People Who Need It, without Getting Paid.
___ I'm the First in Line Putting New Projects Together for Others.
___ I'm Teaching People How to Totally Solve Their Challenges.

___ **COMPASSION:**

___ I'm Taking Care of Others Before They Know They Need Help.
          It Makes Me Drool. lol
___ I'm Making Sure People are Having Balanced Enriching Lives.
___ I'm Going to Great Distance to Making Sure People are Ok,
___ I'm Willing to Travel to Help Others, If My Loved Ones are OK.
___ I'm Teaching Others on How Take Care of Themselves Better.

___ **EXTROVERT:**

___ I'm Getting the Next New Thing that Comes Out to Stick Out.
          It Makes Me Drool. lol
___ I'm in the New Project No One Else can See Right Now?
___ I'm the First to Helping People and Creation if in Need?
___ I'm the First in Line to Go Somewhere New.
___ I'm the First to Help Out Landers Understand the Real Problem?

___ **TEACHING:**

___ I'm Teaching in New Cutting-Edge Ideas.
          It Makes me Drool. lol
___ I'm Teaching in Balanced Ways so Everyone Understands.
___ I'm Teaching Those, others Don't Want to Teach.
___ I'm Teaching in Community Areas others Don't Want to Teach.
___ I'm Teaching Teachers How to Teach.

These are Broad Questions; that cover each of the Five Characteristics, within Each Characteristic.

These Questions Might not be Specific Enough; to Help You Determine a Clear Answer, for Yourself.

As Long as they can trigger an Answer within Yourself; to verify this is One of Your main characteristics, is ALL that matters.

HOW TO DISCOVER MY MAJOR AND MINOR CHARACTERISTICS

Ok now that we know what our two dominate characteristics are. We can now determine, which one is the major and which one is the minor.

This section is going to be the quickest in discovering our majors and miners, IF we have studied all the prior sections before this one.

These verifying questions can and will be applied to all the five characteristics.

If you already know then this can be a verifier.

OK, NOW.... We take the two top characteristics; that got the most check marks, and test them with these questions…

HOW WE FIND and DISCOVER OUR MAJOR CHARACTERISTIC

1. What is the Characteristic that Makes Me Drool? Lol.
2. Am I Honestly Addicted to that Characteristic. No Matter What and When I'm Going Through?
3. And the Oh Yes Bro Question. Am I **THINKING** IT 24/7?

If We Answered YES to All these Questions, Odds are High this is Our Major Characteristic. Again, over time we can get more validation.

HOW WE FIND and DISCOVER OUR MINOR CHARACTERISTIC

1. What is the Characteristic that Makes Me Drool? Lol.
2. Am I Honestly Addicted to that Characteristic. No Matter What and When I'm Going Through?
3. And the Oh Yes Bro Question. Am I **TALKING** IT 24/7?

If We Answered YES to All these Questions, Odds are High this is Our Minor Characteristic. Again, over time we can get more validation.

YUP. Once I **absorb** the Reality that My Major is **THINKING** It 24/7 ALL Naturally, in any situation. ITS THAT EASY.

YUP 2.0 Once I **absorb** the Reality that My Minor is **TALKING** It 24/7 ALL Naturally, in any situation.

CONGRADULATIONS!

Now It's Time to Discover

What Our Major and Minor are

Either Macro and Micro!

OOPS. COMBOS FIRST...
WITH THINKING AND TALKING EXAMPLES

MAJOR AND MINOR CHARACTERISTICS COMBOS

Here is a List of Possible Combos for All Five Characteristics. We'll List Them in Groups Per Characteristic, for Easier Locating.

MAJOR: INSIGHT Big Picture of Subject, Networks and Groups.

MINOR: ACCOUNTABILY Understands the Balanced Details of Subject, Networks and Groups.

> My Major is Always Thinking the Big Picture of Subject, Networks and Groups.
>
> My Minor is Talking the Understanding of the Balanced Details of Big Picture Subject, Networks and Groups. In Relatable Ways to All Five Characteristic Types.

MAJOR: INSIGHT Big Picture of Subject, Networks and Groups.

MINOR: COMPASSION Understands the Details in Having Enriching Relationships Within the Subject, Networks and Groups.

> My Major is Always Thinking the Big Picture of Subject, Networks and Groups.
>
> My Minor is Talking the Understanding of the Details in Having Enriching Relationships Within the Big Picture Subject, Networks and Groups.

MAJOR: INSIGHT Big Picture of Subject, Networks and Groups.

MINOR: EXTROVERT Understands the Details in Connecting Relationships Within the Subject, Networks and Groups.

> My Major is Always Thinking the Big Picture of Subject, Networks and Groups.
>
> My Minor is Talking the Understanding of the Details in Connecting Relationships Within the Big Picture Subject, Networks and Groups.

MAJOR: INSIGHT Big Picture of Subject, Networks and Groups.

MINOR: TEACHING Understands How to Teach the Details in Subject, Networks and Groups.

> My Major is Always Thinking the Big Picture of Subject, Networks and Groups.
>
> My Minor is Talking the Understanding on How to Teach the Details
> in Big Picture Subject, Networks and Groups

MAJOR: ACCOUNTABILITY Understands the Overall Details of Subject, Networks and Groups.

MINOR: SIGHT Sees Details of Subject, Networks and Groups.

> My Major is Always Thinking the Understanding the Overall
> Details of Subject, Networks and Groups.
>
> My Minor is Talking the Visuals in Understanding the Overall
> Details of Subject, Networks and Groups.

MAJOR: ACCOUNTABILITY Understands the Overall Details of Subject, Networks and Groups.

MINOR: COMPASSION Understands the Details in Having Enriching Relationships Within the Subject, Networks and Groups.

> My Major is Always Thinking the Understanding the Overall
> Details of Subject, Networks and Groups.
>
> My Minor is Talking the Understanding of the Details in Having Enriching
> Relationships Within the Overall Details of Subject, Networks and Groups.

MAJOR: ACCOUNTABILITY Understands the Overall Details of Subject, Networks and Groups.

MINOR: EXTROVERT Understands the Details in Connecting Relationships Within the Subject, Networks and Groups.

> My Major is Always Thinking the Understanding the Overall
> Details of Subject, Networks and Groups.
>
> My Minor is Talking the Understanding of the Details in Connecting Relationships
> Within the Overall Details of Subject, Networks and Groups.

MAJOR: ACCOUNTABILITY Understands the Overall Details of Subject, Networks and Groups.

MINOR: TEACHING Understands How to Teach the Details in Subject, Networks and Groups.

> My Major is Always Thinking the Understanding the Overall
> Details of Subject, Networks and Groups.
>
> My Minor is Talking the Understanding on How to Teach the
> Overall Details in Subject, Networks and Groups

MAJOR: COMPASSION Understands the Overall Details in Having Enriching Relationships Within

the Subject, Networks and Groups.

MINOR: INSIGHT Sees Details of Subject, Networks and Groups.

> My Major is Always Thinking the Understanding the Overall Details in Having Enriching Relationships Within the Subject, Networks and Groups.
>
> My Minor is Talking the Visuals in Understanding the Overall Details in Having Enriching Relationships Within the Subject, Networks and Groups.

MAJOR: COMPASSION Understands the Overall Details in Having Enriching Relationships Within the Subject, Networks and Groups.

MINOR: ACCOUNTABILITY Understands the Balanced Details of Subject, Networks and Groups.

> My Major is Always Thinking the Understanding the Overall Details in Having Enriching Relationships Within the Subject, Networks and Groups.

My Minor is Talking the Understanding of the Balanced Details of Having Enriching Relationships Within the Subject, Networks and Groups. In Relatable Ways to All Five Characteristic Types.

MAJOR: COMPASSION Understands the Overall Details in Having Enriching Relationships Within the Subject, Networks and Groups.

MINOR: EXTROVERT Understands the Details in Connecting Relationships Within the Subject, Networks and Groups.

> My Major is Always Thinking the Understanding the Overall Details in Having Enriching Relationships Within the Subject, Networks and Groups.
>
> My Minor is Talking the Understanding of the Overall Details in Connecting Enriching Relationships Within the Subject, Networks and Groups.

MAJOR: COMPASSION Understands the Overall Details in Having Enriching Relationships Within the Subject, Networks and Groups.

MINOR: TEACHING Understands How to Teach the Details in Subject, Networks and Groups.

> My Major is Always Thinking the Understanding the Overall Details in Having Enriching Relationships Within the Subject, Networks and Groups.
>
> My Minor is Talking the Understanding on How to Teach the Overall Details in Having Enriching Relationships Within the Subject, Networks and Groups.

MAJOR: EXTROVERT Understands the Overall Details in Connecting Relationships Within the Subject, Networks and Groups.

MINOR: INSIGHT Sees Details of Subject, Networks and Groups.

My Major is Always Thinking the Understanding of the Overall Details in Connecting Relationships Within the Subject, Networks and Groups.

> My Minor is Talking the Visuals in Understanding the Overall Details in Connecting Relationships Within Subject, Networks and Groups.

MAJOR: EXTROVERT Understands the Overall Details in Connecting Relationships Within the Subject, Networks and Groups.

MINOR: ACCOUNTABILITY Understands the Balanced Details of Subject, Networks and Groups.

My Major is Always Thinking the Understanding of the Overall Details in Connecting Relationships Within the Subject, Networks and Groups.

My Minor is Talking the Understanding of the Overall Balanced Details in Connecting Relationships Within the Subject, Networks and Groups. In Relatable Ways to All Five Characteristic Types.

MAJOR: EXTROVERT Understands the Overall Details in Connecting Relationships Within the Subject, Networks and Groups.

MINOR: COMPASSION Understands the Details in Having Enriching Relationships Within the Subject, Networks and Groups.

> My Major is Always Thinking the Understanding of the Overall Details in Connecting Relationships Within the Subject, Networks and Groups.
>
> My Minor is Talking the Understanding of the Overall Details in Connecting Relationships Within the Overall Details of Subject, Networks and Groups.

MAJOR: EXTROVERT Understands the Overall Details in Connecting Relationships Within the Subject, Networks and Groups.

MINOR: TEACHING Understands How to Teach the Details in Subject, Networks and Groups.

> My Major is Always Thinking the Understanding of the Overall Details in Connecting Relationships Within the Subject, Networks and Groups.
>
> My Minor is Talking the Understanding on How to Teach the Overall Details in Connecting Enriching Relationships Within the Subject, Networks and Groups

MAJOR: TEACHING Understands How to Teach the Overall Details in Subject, Networks and Groups.

MINOR: INSIGHT Sees Details of Subject, Networks and Groups.

> My Major is Always Thinking the Understanding of How to Teach the Overall Details in Subject, Networks and Groups.

> My Minor is Talking the Visuals in Understanding How to Teach the
> Overall Details of Subject, Networks and Groups.

MAJOR: TEACHING Understands How to Teach the Overall Details in Subject, Networks and Groups.

MINOR: ACCOUNTABILITY Understands the Balanced Details of Subject, Networks and Groups.

> My Major is Always Thinking the Understanding of How to Teach the
> Overall Details in Subject, Networks and Groups.

> My Minor is Talking the Understanding of the Balanced Details of How to Teach the Overall Details of Subject, Networks and Groups. In Relatable Ways to All Five Characteristic Types.

MAJOR: TEACHING Understands How to Teach the Overall Details in Subject, Networks and Groups.

MINOR: COMPASSION Understands the Details in Having Enriching Relationships Within the Subject, Networks and Groups.

> My Major is Always Thinking the Understanding of How to Teach the
> Overall Details in Subject, Networks and Groups.

> My Minor is Talking the Understanding of the Details in Having Enriching Relationships Within the Teaching of Overall Details of Subject, Networks and Groups.

MAJOR: TEACHING Understands How to Teach the Overall Details in Subject, Networks and Groups.

MINOR: EXTROVERT Understands the Details in Connecting Relationships Within the Subject, Networks and Groups.

> My Major is Always Thinking the Understanding of How to Teach the
> Overall Details in Subject, Networks and Groups.

> My Minor is Talking the Understanding of the Details in Connecting Relationships Within How to Teach the Overall Details of Subject, Networks and Groups.

SOBERIING NOTE: These Majors and Minors Only Apply to those creatures, that the Unconditional Love part of the Spirit Created.

Self-centered people have a tendency to think people embracing Unconditional Love are delusional.

The creatures and or hijacked Unconditional Love part of the Spirit Creatures; that the Self-Centered Love part of the Spirit created, will have no interested and understanding of the Major and Minor Characteristics.

The Characteristics of the Self-Centered part of the Spirit Are:

NOSIGHT Leads to Panic,

UNCOMMITED Leads to Anger,

HATRED Leads to Revenge,

INTROVERT Leads to Axienty,

and **DOUBT** Leads to Depression.

NOTE: Just because we might have these tendencies from time to time, doesn't mean we are a self-centered person. It means; we are struggling at learning how to be set free, from these characteristics. To Embrace 100% of Who We Are; and Be at Peace with Ourselves, in Unconditional Love.

This is getting TOO deep for this book.

Just noting; to help with these insights, when interacting with self-centered individuals.

At that point; if haven't already, reading the book ETERNALIZING CREATION Final Phase will be a must.

HOW TO DISCOVER MY MACRO AND MICRO CHARACTERISTICS

Ok now that we know, what our major and minor dominate characteristics are. We can now determine the macros and micros of each major and minor characteristics.

This could be the fastest learning and or verifying section in the whole book for you. Lol

Especially if you've absorbed everything before this; and or your major and minor characteristics, are Insight and Accountability.

Ok. Without further due…

Us MACROs. We see the **BIG PICTURE**; Regardless of what's going on, whose saying what and why. It comes ALL Natural. When we're having dreams while sleeping, having a blast and or taking care of our life challenges. *Regardless* if there convenient or not.

Our Macro is **JUST LIKE** our Major, but **MORE INTENSE**. If our Major feels like 100% then our Macros will feel like 1000%.

Us MICROs We see the **FINE DETAILS** of the **SMALL PICTURE**; Regardless of what's going on, whose saying what and why. It comes ALL Natural. When we're having dreams while sleeping, having a blast and or taking care of our life challenges. *Regardless* if their convenient or not.

Our Micro is **JUST LIKE** our Minor, but **MORE INTENSE**. If our Minor feels like 100% then our Micros will feel like 1000%.

NOTE: It can be a **Tad Confusing** between

Majors, Minors, Macros and Micros.

IF IT HELPS

Separate Them into **Two** Different Subjects

KEEP IN MIND;

The Major is what we Predominantly **THINK ALL** the time. Regardless.

The Minor is how we Predominantly **TALK ALL** the time. Regardless.

Now it's Time to Add the Macros and Minors. Think of the Macros and Micros as the **DENSITY** of our Majors and Minors. Macros have more DENSITY than the Micros. Example: If the Macro has a DENSITY of 100% than the Micro has a DENSITY of 50%.

Now Real Time Application. My Major is INSIGHT and its DENSITY is BIG and DEEP, so My Major is at Macro INSIGHT.

If its DENSITY is SMALL and DETAILED then My Major is at Micro INSIGHT.

Another way to looking at Macros and Micros; is like Our Body Parts are Balanced and Co-Dependent, of Each Other. The little ones (micros) are doing all the work, for the greater of the good of the body. And the large ones (macros) are the frame work, in holding the whole body together.

OK, ONE MORE: **The Immediate Now** (TALKING) is more of a Micro Characteristic. **And the No Rush** (THINKING) is more of a Macro Characteristic

That's It. All this knowledge will need to be taken in, at *baby step speeds.*

If this is all overwhelming, then take a break from studying these insights. After the break... Maybe go back in the beginning; and take a nugget or two, and just start working with that insight in your daily life.

Until it comes natural to you to see it, as clear as day. Pat yourself on the back and take another break. When ready find another nugget of interest and apply it to your daily life. Once these insights start to come alive in your life, it will be easier to consume more.

Another suggestion is, just put the book aside period. Get and Read the book ETERNALIZING CREATION Final Phase – if haven't already. Absorb that awareness first. Then more than likely the Rosetta Stone of Unconditional Love; will mean that much more to you and your loved ones.

EITHER WAY. ENJOY!

MAXIMIZING ORGANIZATION'S POTENTIAL

The is where organizations will thrive at the Nth Degree. As we move into the Final Phase of Creation, Employee own organizations will be all the rage. See ETERNALING CREATION Final Phase by Optimum Vizhan, for the Core details. *Summary Version:* Employees know what to do and how to do it best – because they are doing it, verses "managers." Eliminate the "Overhead" and give that portion to the employees through paychecks and or stock into the organization. It would be like their personal retirement fund.

Now we add this knowledge, of matching the individual's major and minor characteristics to the Task. And BAM. The Organization is Now in Maximum Efficiency and Growth Mode, on Steroids. *Without running off the tracks.*

If they are missing individual major and minor characteristics for the Task(s) at hand; then we put in the next best individual, until another one is found to replace.

Knowing this knowledge; also allows the organization to better vet, new people coming into the organization. This is a WIN WIN and a PLUS PLUS; for the organization and the new individual, coming into the organization. They know upfront the new individual's major and minor characteristics. The two-week trial period job results, will verify their major and minor characteristics. The new employee will love their new job off the bat. Saving both time and money at the same time. FOR BOTH.

This goes for any organization.

Especially if the Organization has an individual; who has a Major as INSIGHT and a Minor as ACCOUNTABLITY, running the organization.

Who understands this knowledge; and knows how to find the individual(s) Major and Minor characteristics, by asking a few questions.

The rest will put the organization on auto pilot; without having to stop periodically, to having meetings to figure out the ***whys we's ain't*** going nowhere. Lol.

If don't have someone like that running the organization, and…

If interested in helping your organization move forward into this direction; then feel free to contact the business side of me, at worldwideconnextions.com

I check my emails regularly, but don't answer them all. Unless you give me specifics. Example: This is Me, My Organization, My Email and Phone Number, Best Time to Contact Me, Where We Are at in the Organization and Where We Want to Go Info. Then I will seriously review your information, and get back with you either way.

FRONT COVER

I've always been fascinated with running water over rocks. Especially in the woods. The life it brings to the creation nearby. Growing up on the farm and working the land. I was told rocks grow while their covered with soil. So; when our plows would hit a stone, we would dig it out and set in a pile. Or as landscaping around the farm house. This was like a three-fold decision. One, it would save time next time plowing. Two, prevent damage to the plow next time. Three, rocks make good highlights in landscaping.

Ok. Enough of the background info. It is fascinating to know; rocks grow when in the right environment. They get stronger and stronger. They get bigger and bigger. So, to with our lives.

The Five Characteristics of Unconditional Love; is the environment that allows our life journey, to grow stronger and stronger. With ourselves, our loved ones and with all of creation around us. At times it doesn't "feel" like it, but deep down we all hunger for it.

Oh, one last one. I favored this front cover photo; I created with Canva AI, without realizing there were 5 water fall steps in this small creek/river. Yup. At the very top it appears to be a small one, next one down a little bigger, etc. Each Step gets bigger, than the last one. Each one important. And each one building on the previous one.

Ok. Here's where the tingling sensations came in. The first step seems small; but it's where our physical lives started, as a child. Yep. From this looking back view; appears to be small but it has all that water and life behind it, to create this creek/river journey. The next step down represents our Adult life. The next step down represents our Friendship Life, then our Companion Life and last our Parenting Life.

All those enriching experiences accumulated; allows us to have the honor and privilege, of procreating life. When going through that procreating experience. We can get a taste of how and what the Unconditional Love part of the Spirit; was experiencing when it created us and creation, as eternal friends. It's awesome to think that the Unconditional Love part of the Spirit loves us so much. That it carefully and gently created all these five phases. So that we would understand and appreciate our friendship with ourselves; with Unconditional Love part of the Spirit and all of creation, in deeper and enriching ways.

BACK COVER

The OV Logo was inspired by; the precept of what I see guides me in the direction I go, be it mentally or physically. The healthier the vision the healthier the outcome. **PLUS,** plus. It's actually the roots of how healthy, and big the tree of vision will be. In this case, the passion of seeing all of creation in harmony with each other. To the point there is no more fear of: panicking, anger, revenge, anxiety and depression. Suttle signs of pending conflicts. ALL GONE. We can all lay down, without no fear of. The deeper our roots go, the stronger and bigger the tree can grow.

Oh. And one extra tidbit I learned from growing fruit trees, fruit bushes and annuals like asparagus. The base of the plant, where stem is above ground and the roots are below ground. This base structure will determine the overall health of the plant. The thicker and bigger it can get, the stronger the tree can be. Soooo. When planting them. *Put a heap* of coconut husk underneath the plant's base. This will retain moisture longer, for the base to absorb and strengthen itself.

Now with this environment, the plants will be stronger and provide more fruit. The same with the ROSETTA STONE of Unconditional Love. The ROSETTA STONE of Unconditional Love is the base foundation; for Our Lives to grow stronger and bear more fruit for ourselves, our loved ones and the Creation Around Us. *Awe... Another deep nugget of inspiration.*

It's Time to Embrace Seeing More to Living More Enriching Lives; in Our Friendship Journey in this Final Phase and beyond, with ALL of Creation. Together!

IN CLOSING

As the individual creature and creation
senses are restored
throughout the Final Phase;
they will obtain
their complete memory
of their journey,
from the beginning in the womb
of the Unconditional Love
part of the Spirit
to current.

My Awareness to This Journey Started with Max; and has been accelerating every day, after Max's Transitioning on 09-13-2022…

NOW IT'S TIME, TO ENJOY OUR
UNCONDITIONAL LOVE JOURNEY!

ABOUT THE AUTHOR

Optimum Vizhan   Ov - See More Live More!

Grew up on a small farm. Enjoying and Love attending the horses, rabbits, cats, roosters, chickens and my dog smug. Worked as a team with my dad; working, planting and harvesting the land crops. Invented a horse manure from old lawn mower parts; to sell shredded clumps of horse manure, out by the road. Produced an Old School Block Buster Short Film for Family. Basement packed with people, demanded to see it three times. Married. Three beautiful children. Divorced. Single Parent for 13+ yrs with zero help from ex. Shipping and Receiving Supervisor for 35+ yrs. Set up and maintain supply chain for five locations. Set Up Distribution Center to Supply the 19 Locations for the USPS, coast to coast USA. As a fill Plant Mgr for 3 months; changed manufacturing work centers into a more efficient way. Faster, Easier and Added another work center in the mix. Employees loved it so much, demanded returning Plant Mgr NOT to changed anything back. Authored and Published: Maximizing the Armor of God, His Life manuscript, New Friendship Bible meditations, Can My Life Change, The Presidents Apocalypse, Hell and Back, Gravity and Motion, My Hell and Back 103 Survival Tips. PLUS: Learning how to Master Self-Publishing with my two new books: My Hell and Back 103 Survival Tips Plus and Eternalizing Creation final phase.

www.ingramcontent.com/pod-product-compliance
Lightning Source LLC
Chambersburg PA
CBHW041702160426
43202CB00002B/11